Beyond The Rainbow
A Passionate Tale Of Children And Animals
Who Meet In The Spirit World

Ebook ISBN: 978-1-7351076-8-4
Print Book ISBN: 978-1-7351076-7-7

Dedication

- Dedicated to my angel sister Tammy, whose life was taken so young; my *Sister of the Rain* who communicates frequently from the other side.
- To my parents who found the strength to carry on for years and years and years after that tragic night.
- To my surviving sister who gracefully carries the weight of the world; my rock and source of love and laughter while growing up.
- To my spouse, best-friend and life partner who made this book a reality through her encouragement, infinite love, and technical support.
- To those who see me as 'Amazing Amy', family and friends alike, who steadily encourage me to "Use My Wings."

Beyond the Rainbow 🌈

The Storm Before the Rainbow

On November 20th, 1981, our world was turned upside down when the police delivered the tragic news that my sister, Tammy, had died in a car accident. She was just 17 years old and a senior in high school. At that time, my mother was on a business trip, and I distinctly remember making that dreadful call. The heart-wrenching cries of a mother mourning her child will forever be etched in my memory. Although I wasn't there to witness my father and step-mother's reactions, I can only imagine it was equally devastating.

From the other side, Tammy quickly learned to communicate with us…The day of her funeral was marked by an unexpected and massive snowstorm, with drifts accumulating three feet deep on the roads. Nonetheless, this did not hinder the funeral, where we witnessed a unprecedented turnout at the church, followed by a procession that stretched five miles to the cemetery. At the cemetery, the pallbearers, dressed impeccably in their Sunday best, had to push the hearse and limousines through the snow. We all felt that Tammy was making her presence known with that unusual snowstorm.

This was further confirmed during her graveside service when a large mass of snow tumbled from a nearby 40-foot pine tree, landing directly on the pastor! Laughter erupted from everyone present. That single moment of laughter is a cherished memory for our family, that continues to bring us joy in our grief.

Since that day, Tammy continues to communicate with us regularly, often through white feathers found in unexpected places - like on an airplane seat, and through unusual rain events - especially on our moving days over the years. We eventually understood that Tammy was reminding us that it's "just stuff."

Due to her frequent messages via the weather, I affectionately refer to her as Titaua: My "Sister of The Rain" or "Sister of Heaven," inspired by a beautiful Tahitian woman we once met in Papeete.

Tammy's favorite message to send, centers around the number 11. With her birthday falling on August 11th, we frequently see 8:11 on clocks, both morning and night. However, the number we encounter most often is 11:11. Also known as an angel number, 11:11 signifies the presence of angelic energies nearby. Each time we see 11:11, we know Tammy is close, which happens ALL THE TIME! Adding to her messages involving the number 11, I often find coins, typically a penny and a dime together. Over the years, I have collected these coins and placed them on our front doormat for good blessings to all who enter. The doormat is now covered!

One of the most memorable finds occurred during a remarkable moment when I attended a live event with Theresa Caputo, the Long Island Medium, in Denver. In a venue filled with 6,500 people, I discovered a dime and a penny beneath my assigned seat. At that moment, I realized I wouldn't receive a connection that night, because I had already received my message from Tammy; and others at the event needed Theresa's mediumship far more than I did.

This is only the beginning of the story...

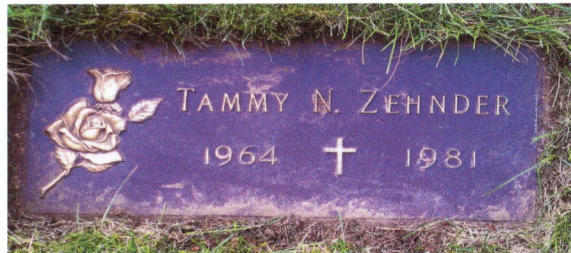

TAMMY N. ZEHNDER
1964 ✝ 1981

August 11, 1964 - November 20, 1981

Fast forward 42 years: This book began to take shape on the anniversary of Tammy's passing, November 20th, 2023. While driving across the country to celebrate Thanksgiving with my Dad and Stepmom in Tennessee, I asked Tammy to appear to me as we slept in our camper van. Having never done something like this before, I was uncertain of what to expect or if she would even show up. I was in a trance-like state when she appeared before me, radiating beauty and grace.

Tammy, in that moment, embodied a Disney-style princess, complete with her long blonde hair and blue eyes. She hovered above me, smiling gracefully, and expressed that she was happy and busy. When I mentally asked her, "What keeps you busy?" She revealed a comprehensive "first moments in heaven" program that she manages, based on her own transition.

Upon her sudden arrival in heaven, she too experienced a moment of bewilderment and an unfamiliar, surreal sensation regarding what had just happened. Although it was heavenly, it took a moment to realize what just transpired. Over time, she noticed that pets and animals arrive with the same split second of bewilderment and wonder.

Having grown up on a farm, Tammy also understood the profound bond between a child and a pet; a heartfelt connection that brings immediate joy. Her heavenly program was designed to pair children (of all ages) with animals and pets (of any kind) upon their arrival in the next realm.

This pairing magically alleviates their anxiety and brings joy to their hearts during their transition.

Heidi, Amy, & Tammy with a lion cub
1969

I was astonished by the vivid and real images Tammy presented to me that night. I expressed my gratitude for her sharing her world with me and eventually drifted off to sleep in a daze, with tears streaming down my cheeks.

The next day, I documented the moment but I have never referred back to my notes, as the images were etched in my mind. About a year later, Tammy inspired me to write this book. I asked for her assistance to make it happen, and the following day, a poem flowed effortlessly from my fingertips. Months later, I began to create images with the help of AI. Though I am an artist and a painter, these images were essential in bringing this book to life in a realistic timeframe.

I hope that this is the book that you never have to read, but now that you are here; I hope you find this inspired story comforting and a source of peace for you, or anyone you know, who is experiencing the loss of a loved one or pet. I believe it will help the grieving process, while capturing beautiful memories of loved ones who are never truly gone. They appear frequently to remind us that they are at peace and still near us every day.

In fact, Tammy is here right now on the day of her book being published, November 20, 2025, because once again, after months of drought, it is snowing. ❄️

Live, Love, Laugh,
Amy "Doc" Z.

Pictured above (left to right):
Tammy in Hawai'i 1981
AI image of Tammy with her childhood pets
Tammy's Senior Photo

The Story Begins...

This is a story about the little ones,
The dear ones, and the furry-scurry ones.

Who depart this earth way too soon,
Destined to meet, on the other side of the moon.

This is a story about every little one;
Whose hearts have longed, for animal fun.

A story about, unconditional love.
The kind you only get,
From having something to hug.

Heart to heart, giggles and laughs;
The perfect match, one made to last.

Now, stop right there. I'm a little confused,
What is going on here? Although I'm bemused.

Some children, who have lived on this earth,
Have wanted a pet to love, since birth.

Be it furry or slithery, big or small;
An animal to love, with kisses and all!

For a variety of reasons, however unfair,
Some children pass early, they run out of air.

One thing we know, without a doubt,
They arrive in heaven,
When their time runs out.

Some have had time, to say goodbye,
Others arrive quickly,
And don't know why.

While those at home are distraught and sad,
The child is paired,
With a pet they never had.

Now here's the twist, that you may not have seen,
The animals who pass,
Come from a similar scene.

They too, have had a tough go...

Some abused, some sick,
Some young, some old,
No matter the reason, they were all so bold.

What they need and want is the same as you,
The comfort of knowing,
Their new friend is true.

Immediately, upon their arrival in heaven.
The match is made, to relieve any tension.

The child receives, their dream animal friend,
So that they both can immediately,
Be on the mend.

Along with comfort, to which both souls cling,
They are each adorned,
With beautiful wings.

Upon which they ride, with no limits at all.
Up, up and away, no fears, no falls.

Only joy in their hearts, and a smile on their face,
For these souls have won, the happiness race.

But for souls left behind,
Your fears come to life,
The pain is so deep, it cuts like a knife.

Find comfort in knowing,
Your loved ones are free,
They now have a companion, and a flying degree!

This story's not over,
There's more you should know.
It's my sister in heaven, who runs this whole show!

She grew up on a farm,
With animals so near,...

But her young life was taken,
So sudden, oh dear!

When years later, I asked her to show me her face,
She appeared in an instant,
With beauty and grace.

I asked her to show me what fills up her days,
She showed me this program,
Was I in a daze?

She said that it's real,
And there's no better deal.

She said when they arrive,
She shares what's in store.
A bundle of love, who awaits at the door.

For there's no bigger love, for each one to get,
Than the one that is instant,
Between child and pet.

From giggles, to kisses, to hugs oh so tight,
From furry to lizards, whatever feels right.

For anyone preparing to cross that big bridge,
Think of a pet that awaits you at the ridge.

If you are wondering,
"Is this program for me?"
The answer is, Yes! When your soul is set free.

For anyone grieving, the loss of a soul,
Just ask them to show you,
Which pet met their goal...

...And for those of you wondering,
Where your pet went?
They too, can show you their pairing, upon ascent.

11:11

For souls are very smart cookies, you see.
They communicate daily, with you and me.

You can sit in the silence,
With your eyes closed tight,
And imagine their face, their eyes, their light.

They will come sit beside you,
And whisper in your ear,
"I am happy, I'm safe, I'm flying up here!"

One more thing to share,
Is to look for the signs,
That our loved one's send, to those left behind.

A feather, a penny, a rock shaped like a heart,
Never doubt, that our loved ones are smart!
(Even pets!)

When my writing was finished,
Much to my shock,
There was a message from heaven, 11:11 o'clock!

About the Authors

Meet CCnDoc! The unapologetically eclectic dynamic duo bringing digital creations as well as books on coaching, financial education, nature, spiritual endeavors & more, to kids of all ages.

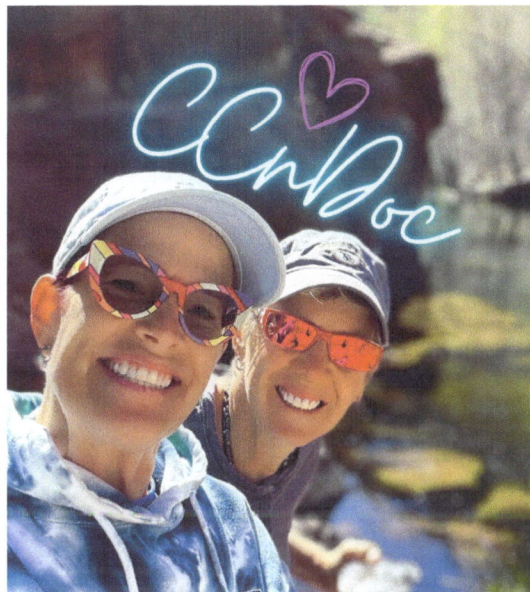

After 25-years of business travel and adventures all over the globe, this life-loving, nature-exploring couple, experienced a life changing transformation - a cancer diagnosis - that led them deep into an exploration of the spiritual world and the discovery gifts they didn't realize they had. This book is just one result of that quest...

Learning how much healing comes from Mind-Body-AND-Spirt work, integrated with traditional medicine, they embarked on a spiritual journey that opened their eyes and minds to unimaginable possibilities. This awakening, along with a powerful vision and channeling from a sister on the other side, paved the way for the creation of this book.

Visit them at CCnDoc.com or @CCnDoc on social media.
Please note, not all CCnDoc content is made for young children.

Other titles:
- 🌈 *Courageous Money: Your Adventure Through Money National Park*
- 🌈 *The Big Book of Southern Colorado Wildflowers: For Kids of All Ages*
- 🌈 *Connecting With Spirit: Mind, Body & Soul*
- 🌈 *Coaching For Commitment Simplified: A Supplemental Guide for Leaders & Coaches*